EXPLORING THE HUMAN BODY

Reproduction and Growth

Michaela Miller

KIDHAVEN PRESS
An imprint of Thomson Gale, a part of The Thomson Corporation

THOMSON

GALE

Detroit • New York • San Francisco • San Diego • New Haven, Conn. • Waterville, Maine • London • Munich

Produced by Arcturus Publishing Ltd,
26/27 Bickels Yard, 151–153 Bermondsey Street, London SE1 3HA

© 2005 Arcturus Publishing

Series concept: Alex Woolf
Editor: Alex Woolf
Designer: Peta Morey
Artwork: Michael Courtney
Picture researcher: Glass Onion Pictures
Consultant: Dr Kristina Routh

For more information, contact
KidHaven Press
27500 Drake Rd.
Farmington Hills, MI 48331-3535
Or you can visit our Internet site at http://www.gale.com

Picture Credits
Corbis: 29 (Gideon Mendel).
La Leche League International: 20 (Suba Tidball).
Science Photo Library: 5 (Lea Paterson), 7 (BSIP, Laurent), 11 (Dr Yorgos Nikas), 13 (Ian Boddy), 15 (Dr G. Moscoso), 17 (Deep Light Productions), 18 (Ruth Jenkinson/MIDIRS), 21 (Ian Hooton), 23 (BSIP, Laurent), 25 (Damien Lovegrove), 26 (Tek Image), 27 (BSIP, Laurent), 28 (Eye of Science).
Topfoto: 24 (John Powell).

LIBRARY OF CONGRESS CATALOGING-IN-PUBLICATION DATA

Miller, Michaela, 1961–
    Reproduction and growth / by Michaela Miller.
        p. cm. — (Exploring the human body)
    Includes bibliographical references and index.
    ISBN 0-7377-3021-8 (hardcover : alk. paper)
    1. Human reproduction—Juvenile literature. 2. Birth—Juvenile literature. I. Title. II. Series.
    QP251.5.M554 2005
    612.6—dc22
                                                            2004023352

Printed in Singapore

Contents

Creating Life

If living things stopped reproducing—creating new life—the world would become an empty place. All types of life, including plants, animals, and bacteria, would soon die out.

Different creatures reproduce in different ways. The smallest creatures, like amoebae, simply split in half to create more amoebae. This way of reproducing is called asexual reproduction. Other living things need two sexes—a male and a female—to join together, before new life can be created. This is called sexual reproduction.

Hatching or Birth?

Just as different creatures have different ways of reproducing, their babies have different ways of entering the world as well. Female mammals, such as humans, grow their babies inside their bodies until the babies are ready to be born. Most other animals, like birds, fish, amphibians, reptiles, and insects, lay eggs. Their young develop in the eggs until they are ready to hatch.

Human Reproduction

Human reproduction, or sex, often seems more complicated than reproduction for the rest of the animal kingdom. This is because humans are highly complex and social creatures, and the way they go about reproducing usually involves strong feelings and emotions. Love, attraction, care, and respect are just some of the positive feelings that can be associated with human reproduction.

This diagram shows asexual reproduction. An amoeba—a single-celled creature—simply splits in two when it reaches a certain size.

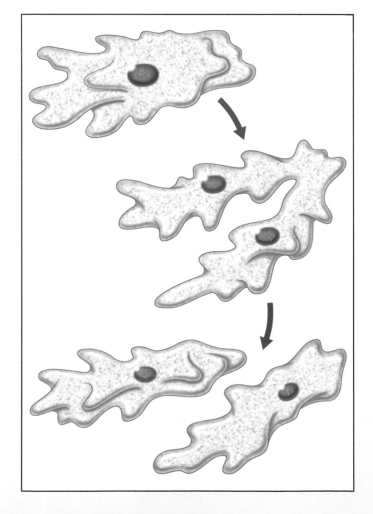

Human babies are produced through sexual reproduction.

As children grow up and enter puberty—when their bodies become sexually mature—they usually find themselves thinking more about sex and asking questions about it. This is completely normal—if they did not have these feelings or curiosity, the human race would soon cease to exist.

However, like many other things, reproduction can have a negative side, too. If people do not look after their bodies, they can become ill and pass on diseases through having sex. If babies are born to parents who do not want them or cannot care for them properly, the babies will suffer and may even die. Also, if someone has sex before they are ready, they can feel bad too.

Case notes

How long does it take to reproduce?

The length of time it takes to reproduce depends on the type of animal. Human babies usually take around forty weeks to grow inside their mothers before they are ready to be born. An elephant pregnancy can last two years. Bird eggs can take anywhere between two and eleven weeks to hatch, depending on the type of bird. Eggs from small birds take less time to hatch than eggs from large birds like an ostrich.

The Female Reproductive System

To reproduce, both females and males have reproductive organs. A woman's reproductive organs are tucked inside her body. They are connected to an opening between her legs called the vagina, or birth canal. The vagina is between two other openings: the anus, from which solid waste (feces) leaves the body, and the urethra, which lets liquid waste (urine) out.

The female reproductive organs also include two ovaries, two fallopian tubes and a uterus—also known as a womb. Each of these parts is needed to create life.

Ovaries are two rounded organs, about 1.18 inches (3cm) long, that store hundreds of thousands of tiny eggs. These eggs are the female sex cells. Each egg—called an ovum—is about as big as a pencil dot. Although a girl's ovaries store hundreds of thousands of eggs, only about four hundred will be released during her lifetime.

The Egg's Journey

Before a baby can start to form, an ovum must travel along a fallopian tube and successfully join with a male sex cell called a sperm. This joining is known as fertilization.

This diagram shows how the female reproductive system is situated within the body.

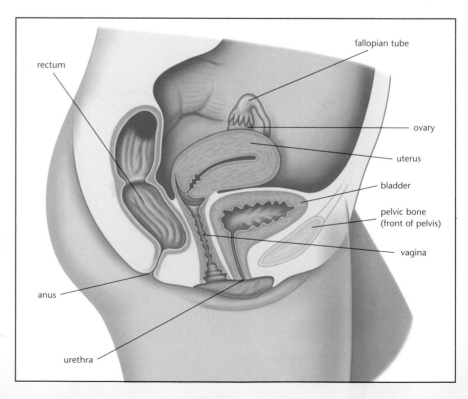

Eggs only start to be released when the female reproductive organs are mature enough. This happens when a girl reaches puberty—usually in her early teens. Chemicals in her blood, known as hormones, tell the ovaries to release one egg. After that, an egg will be released each month, usually from alternate ovaries.

Before the egg is released, the uterus gets ready for the possible arrival of a fertilized egg by making a soft lining that is rich in blood vessels. If the egg is not fertilized, the lining is not needed. It breaks down, with the egg, into a few tablespoons of blood and leaves the body through the vagina.

Sometimes menstruation causes pain. Exercise, heat, and pain-killing medicine can help, but anyone worried about period pain should see her doctor.

This bleeding happens about every 28 days and is called menstruation, or a period. During periods, girls and women usually use sanitary napkins or tampons to stop the blood from getting on their underwear. Most women stop menstruating when they reach about fifty years old, and they are no longer fertile. This is called menopause.

Case notes

When do periods start?

Most girls start menstruating between the ages of eleven and thirteen, but some may start their periods as early as nine or as late as fifteen. This is normal. Periods last from about three to eight days and usually happen every month, but they can happen more or less often than that.

The Male Reproductive System

The male reproductive organs—the penis and the testes (or testicles)—are outside a man's body and hang between his legs. The two testes are held and protected by a bag of skin called the scrotum.

Each testicle produces sperm—the male sex cells—usually beginning when a boy is between ten and twelve years old. The scrotum's job is to keep the testes at the right temperature for sperm production. In the cold, the scrotum moves the testes close to the body to keep the sperm warm. In the heat it moves them farther away from the body to keep the sperm cool.

Sperm are tiny cells visible only with a microscope. They have a tadpole shape, with a round head and long tail. Each sperm is about $\frac{2}{1000}$ inch (0.05mm) long. The testes produce millions of sperm every day.

The Sperm's Journey

For reproduction to take place, sperm have to leave the body through the penis. To get there they first have to travel from the testes through a series of tubes. Each testicle

This diagram shows how the male reproductive system is situated within the body.

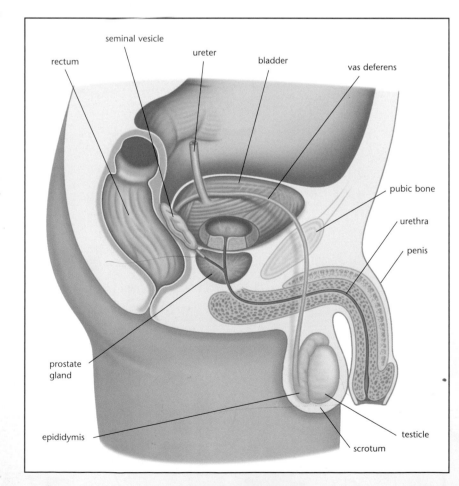

seminal vesicle

rectum

ureter

bladder

vas deferens

pubic bone

urethra

penis

prostate gland

epididymis

testicle

scrotum

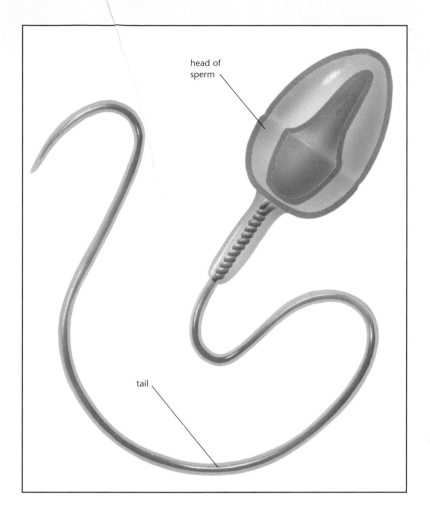

head of
sperm

tail

This drawing shows a highly magnified sperm. The head of the sperm, which joins with the egg, is moved along by the tail.

has its own set of tubes. The first set is called the epididymis, which acts as a sperm storage area. The sperm then travel through the next set of tubes, known as the vas deferens. Here they start mixing with fluids produced by the seminal vesicles and the prostate gland. This mixture of fluid and sperm is called semen.

The semen travels up through a tube in the penis called the urethra before emerging rapidly through an opening at the tip of the penis. This is called ejaculation and usually happens only when the penis is hard. This hardness is known as an erection and it happens when men are sexually excited.

The urethra also connects to the bladder where urine is stored, but special muscles ensure that during an erection and ejaculation, urine and semen do not come out of the urethra at the same time.

Case notes

What is a wet dream?

Wet dreams are a common sign that a boy has reached puberty, and that his body is now producing sperm. During a wet dream a boy is normally dreaming of something that makes him sexually excited. He then has an erection and ejaculates semen, which makes his sheets or pajamas wet and sticky.

Creating a Baby

Before an egg can be fertilized and a baby created, a man's penis and a woman's vagina must join together. This joining is called sexual intercourse, sex, or making love. Sexual intercourse usually happens privately when a man and woman feel very close and attracted to one another.

During sex, the man's penis becomes hard and erect and the woman's vagina becomes wet and slippery so that the penis can slide easily inside her. The man and woman then move together so that the penis slides in and out of the vagina.

This movement encourages the sperm and semen to start moving through the network of tubes in the man's scrotum and penis. Eventually the man's penis ejaculates and the semen enters the woman's vagina.

The Sperm Race

Each ejaculation contains between 2 and 5 million sperm. They all swim quickly, using their tadpolelike tails, to go up the vagina, into the uterus and toward the fallopian tube. Each sperm races to join with the egg, or ovum. If they find the egg, the sperm surround it and try to burrow in to fertilize it. Only one sperm will be successful and join with the egg to start a new life.

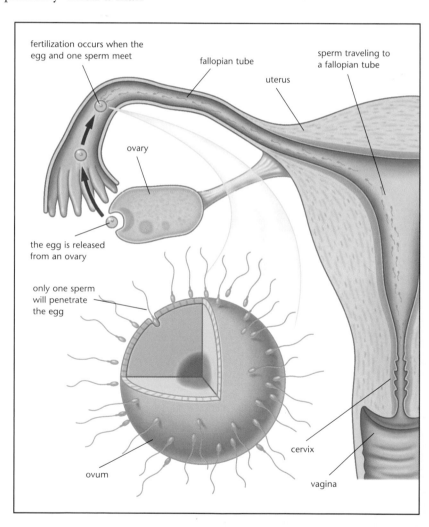

fertilization occurs when the egg and one sperm meet

fallopian tube

sperm traveling to a fallopian tube

uterus

ovary

the egg is released from an ovary

only one sperm will penetrate the egg

cervix

ovum

vagina

How a new life begins. This diagram shows how sperm travel through the cervix and uterus and into a fallopian tube to fertilize an egg.

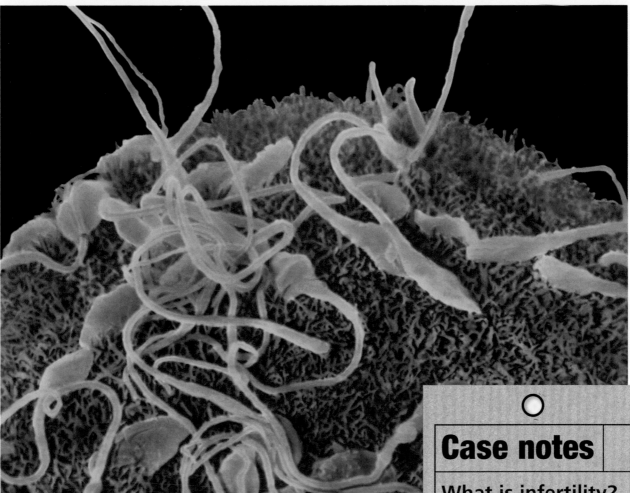

Only one sperm out of the millions released can join with the egg and start a new life.

Not all the sperm, however, surround the egg. This is because the egg releases a chemical that can attract only about two hundred sperm. Out of these two hundred, only one sperm will join with the egg.

Life is not started every time a man and woman have sexual intercourse. Reproduction only happens if a sperm joins with an egg within twenty-four to thirty-six hours of the egg leaving the ovary for the fallopian tube. Any later than this and the egg is too old. It will simply break down and come out of the woman's body during her period.

Case notes

What is infertility?

Sometimes, despite having sexual intercourse, people cannot reproduce and are described as infertile. The reasons for this can be quite complicated, but usually have to do with the reproductive organs not working properly. Scientists and doctors have been able to help some couples who seem infertile to reproduce. Some people, however, are never able to have their own children. This can be very upsetting for them.

Genes and Chromosomes

Eggs and sperm carry important information and instructions. When the egg and sperm meet at fertilization to form a new life, this information determines how the baby will look, whether it will be a boy or girl, and how its body will function.

The information about all these things is contained in tiny packages called genes, and they lie on chromosomes. Chromosomes are coiled strands of a chemical called DNA (deoxyribonucleic acid). Each egg and each sperm have twenty-three chromosomes.

During fertilization, the egg and sperm create one cell containing forty-six chromosomes (twenty-three from each parent) and more than one hundred thousand genes. This cell then multiplies into other cells, each one containing the same forty-six chromosomes and their genes.

Genes

Genes decide things like the eye, skin, and hair color of the baby, and how tall he or she will grow. Genes are passed on through families. Besides the genes of its parents, a baby's body will also contain some of the genes of

Each human cell contains forty-six chromosomes, which are made of coiled strands of DNA (deoxyribonucleic acid). Genes lie along the chromosomes.

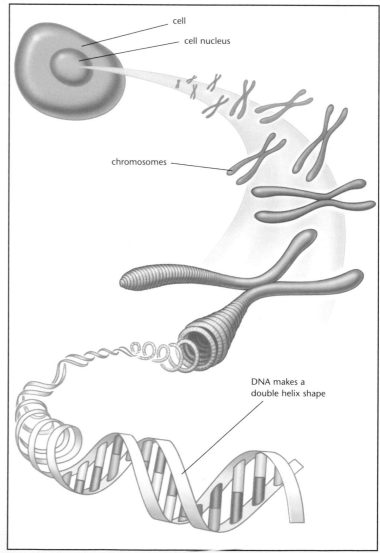

cell

cell nucleus

chromosomes

DNA makes a double helix shape

its grandparents, great-grandparents, and even its ancient ancestors. Genes also determine whether a baby will inherit certain diseases. Diseases like cystic fibrosis, muscular dystrophy, and hemophilia are passed on through families.

The order in which genes and chromosomes are put together is what makes humans unique. No two humans can have the same DNA. The only exceptions to this rule are identical twins (see Case notes).

These identical twins were formed when their mother's egg split in two after being fertilized by the father's sperm.

Boy or Girl?

Eggs and sperm contain a sex chromosome that scientists call X or Y. As soon as an egg and sperm join together, the combination of sex chromosomes they produce decides whether the baby will be a boy or a girl. Eggs can only have the X chromosome, but sperm can have either an X or a Y. If a sperm with an X chromosome joins with the egg, then the baby will be a girl. If a sperm with a Y chromosome joins with the egg, then the baby will be a boy.

Case notes

How are twins made?

There are two types of twins —identical and fraternal. Fraternal, or nonidentical, twins form when two eggs leave the ovary at exactly the same time and are fertilized by two separate sperm. These twins will not look identical and they can be different sexes. Identical twins form if a single egg splits into two after fertilization. These twins will be the same sex, share the same genes, and look the same.

Early Development

After the egg and sperm join, they form one cell. A few hours later this cell divides into two. Then these new cells divide in two to create four cells. All the cells keep dividing over and over again until a ball of cells called a blastocyst is produced.

The blastocyst forms more cells as it travels slowly down the fallopian tube toward the uterus. The journey takes about seven days and the blastocyst will be made up of about one hundred cells when it arrives in the uterus. Once there it floats around for about two days until it finds a place in the uterus's soft lining that it can burrow into.

The center of the blastocyst contains the cells that will eventually grow into the baby. The cells on the outside form a protective layer—a sac of fluid in which the baby will float until it is ready to be born.

Some of the outside cells—those that have joined with the wall of the uterus—also make an organ called the placenta. The placenta provides the baby with all of the food and oxygen it needs while it grows in its mother's uterus. It also provides a way for carbon dioxide and any other waste that the baby produces to leave the mother's

This diagram shows the journey of the fertilized egg to the uterus. As it travels, it turns into a ball of cells called a blastocyst.

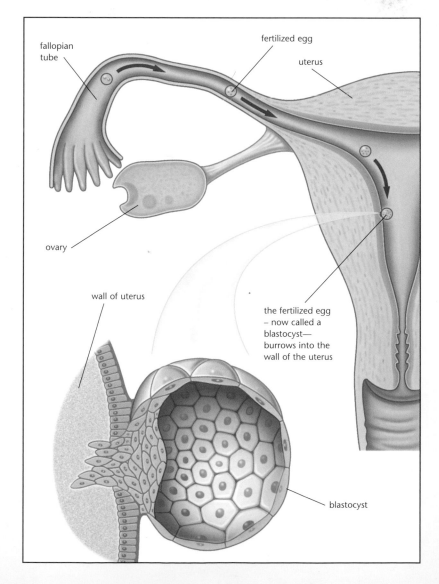

fallopian tube

fertilized egg

uterus

ovary

wall of uterus

the fertilized egg – now called a blastocyst—burrows into the wall of the uterus

blastocyst

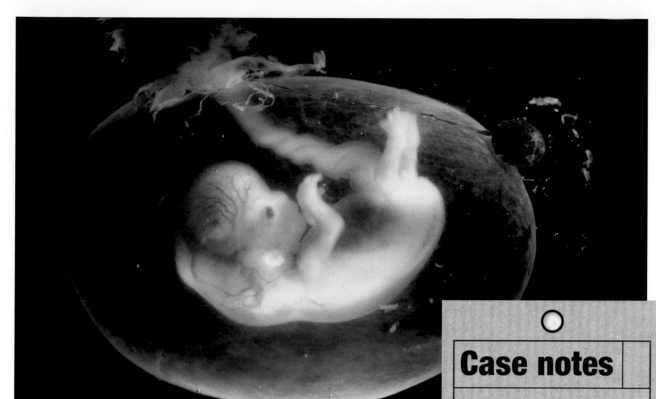

This embryo is seven or eight weeks old. It is just 1.57 inches (4cm) long, but its eyes and limbs are already formed.

body through her bloodstream. The baby is connected to the placenta by a cord from its abdomen called the umbilical cord.

For the first eight weeks of its life inside its mother, doctors and scientists usually call the baby an embryo. After eight weeks and until it is born they call it a fetus.

Changes to the Mother

When a woman is first pregnant there are no signs of anything growing inside her at all. Her body is, however, changing. Her periods will stop and her breasts may feel uncomfortable as they prepare to produce milk. During early pregnancy many women also start to feel nauseated because of the changes their bodies must make for the baby developing inside. This is called morning sickness, although it can happen at any time of the day.

Case notes

What is a miscarriage?

Miscarriages may happen in the first few months of a pregnancy, usually when the embryo or fetus does not form properly and dies. The uterus then pushes the lining and the embryo or fetus into the vagina and out of the body. For some women this can seem like a very heavy and very painful period. A doctor may decide that a simple operation is needed to clear out the uterus completely. Miscarriages can be very upsetting, but most women who have them go on to have healthy babies.

Weeks Eight to Forty

When the fetus is eight weeks old, it measures about 1 inch (2.5cm) long and weighs about one-tenth ounce (2g). Its heart and lungs have formed, and its arms and legs move about. It is also starting to look a little more like a baby.

At twelve weeks it measures about 3 inches (7.5cm) long and weighs about six-tenths ounce (18g). It has ears and eyelids. At this stage, its head is much bigger than its body. As it grows, the fetus spends its days floating in a fluid-filled sac, called the amniotic sac, in the mother's uterus. Here it is kept at the right temperature and is protected from the outside world.

Taking Care

In these early months of pregnancy, the growing baby can be badly affected by diseases that its mother may catch or by any drugs that she may take. Pregnant women are usually told not to smoke, drink alcohol, or take any drugs not recommended by their doctors. They are also often told not to eat certain foods like soft cheeses, shellfish, lightly cooked meat, and eggs because these may contain bacteria that can make both the mother and baby ill.

A woman and fetus in the final week of pregnancy.

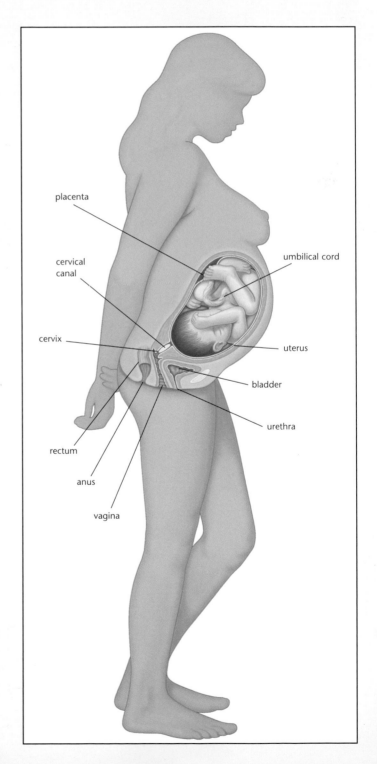

placenta

cervical canal

cervix

rectum

anus

vagina

umbilical cord

uterus

bladder

urethra

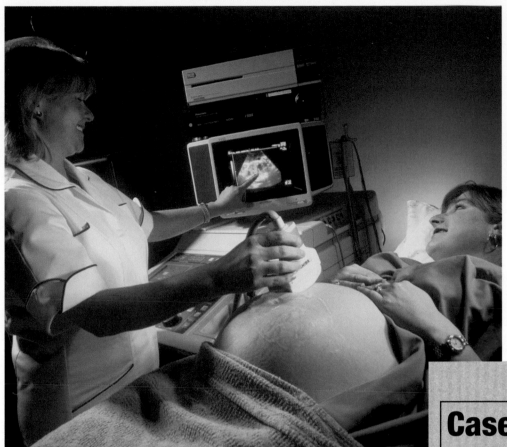

At several stages during her pregnancy, a woman may have ultrasound scans to check that the baby is growing normally.

The Developing Fetus

Between sixteen and twenty weeks, the baby grows very quickly and its mother's shape changes. She starts to look rounder and pregnant. At about twenty weeks she will probably feel the baby move. At this stage, the baby will be about 10 inches (25cm) long. It kicks and somersaults in its amniotic sac, and its heartbeat can be heard through a stethoscope. Its sex organs are now also big enough to tell whether it is a boy or a girl.

At forty weeks, most babies are ready to be born. Most of them turn upside down so that their heads are facing downwards toward the cervix (the opening at the bottom of the uterus). Some babies are born before thirty-seven weeks and are called premature babies. If they are born very early, they will need special care at a hospital.

○

Case notes

What is an ultrasound scan?

Ultrasound scans show doctors how the unborn baby is developing within its mother's uterus. Scans use high-pitched sound waves that bounce off the baby and make a picture. From the picture, doctors can take measurements that show whether the baby is growing normally. Sometimes, if the baby is in the right position, they can even tell if it is a boy or a girl. Ultrasound scans do not harm the mother or the baby.

Giving Birth

Birth starts when hormones in a pregnant woman's blood send a message to the uterus saying it is time for the baby to be born. This message tells the uterus to tighten and squeeze its strong muscles and make a pushing motion called a contraction.

Contractions work together to push the baby out of its mother's body. The time from when the contractions start to when the baby is finally born is called labor. Labor is another name for work.

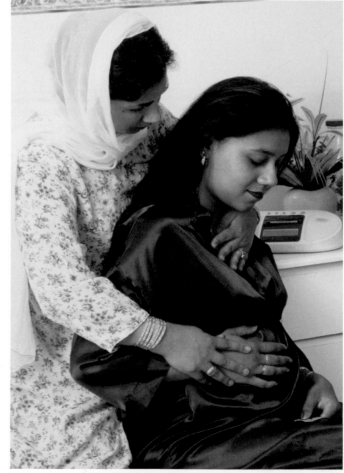

During labor many women like to have the support of their friends and family.

Hard Work

When labor starts, contractions are weak and spaced far apart. As time goes on they start getting stronger and closer together. It can take just a few hours or several days for a baby to be born. The pains the contractions cause are known as labor pains.

The contractions push the baby's head from the uterus into the cervix. The cervix opens up. It gets wider and wider until it eventually lets the baby's head enter the mother's vagina—the birth canal. The vagina then stretches to let the baby out of its mother's body.

During the contractions, a midwife or obstetrician will encourage the mother to push downwards to help the baby out. Sometimes babies need more help leaving their mothers' bodies. They have to be pulled out with forceps, which look a little like salad tongs, or a ventouse extractor—a suction cup.

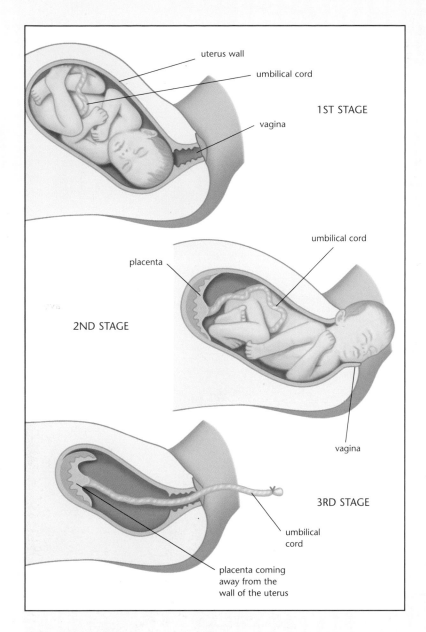

uterus wall

umbilical cord

1ST STAGE

vagina

umbilical cord

placenta

2ND STAGE

vagina

3RD STAGE

umbilical cord

placenta coming away from the wall of the uterus

The three stages of labor.

First Breaths

Once a baby is born, it normally takes its first breath and starts to cry. These cries help make the baby breathe and take oxygen from the air instead of from the placenta and umbilical cord.

When the baby finally leaves the vagina, the doctor or midwife clamps and cuts the umbilical cord. This separates the baby from the placenta, which at this point is usually still inside the mother's body. Meanwhile the contractions continue until the placenta and the rest of the umbilical cord are pushed out.

Case notes

What is a cesarean?

Sometimes babies are born by cesarean section. This is an operation where the mother is first given an injection to stop her from feeling any pain. The surgeon then makes a side-to-side cut low down on the mother's abdomen into the uterus. The baby and placenta are taken out gently and the cut is stitched or stapled up. Cesareans usually happen if doctors think the mother will have problems giving birth or if they are worried about the health of the baby.

A Baby's First Year

Most newborn babies are about 20 inches (50cm) long and weigh about six or seven pounds (between 3 and 3.5 kg).

They can see and hear and will cry when hungry, thirsty, or uncomfortable. Babies are also born, like all mammals, with the ability to suckle milk from their mothers. This suckling action is called a reflex—something that is done automatically. If a baby's face is lightly stroked near its mouth it turns its head to one side and opens its mouth. This reflex helps the baby find its mother's breast or a bottle and start feeding.

Breastfeeding is a natural way of feeding babies. Breast milk provides all the nutrients a baby needs to be healthy.

Feeding Time

Newborn babies' digestive systems are not able to deal with solid food, so mothers produce milk in their breasts for the babies to drink. When a newborn baby first sucks at its mother's breast, the hormones in her body tell the breasts to start producing milk. The first liquid produced is called colostrum, which is very thick and full of nutrients. After two or three days, breast milk then appears. This milk contains all the nutrients a baby needs to be healthy. It also contains the mother's immunities—protection from disease—and can keep the baby from getting ill.

Not all mothers choose to breastfeed their babies. Companies make and sell baby formula milk from cow's milk, which can be fed to babies from a bottle. After six months, most babies are slowly introduced to solid food.

This baby is six months old. He can only stand with help, but in six more months he will probably be walking on his own.

Case notes

How do babies learn to talk?

No one is really sure why or how a baby learns to talk. Some scientists think babies learn by being around other people, listening to them and copying them. Other scientists think that the brain is made so that we talk at some stage automatically. Most toddlers are using simple words when they are between twelve and eighteen months of age.

Growing Babies

Babies that are healthy and well cared for grow and develop skills. At three months old most will hold up their heads and make noises when they are talked to. They also like to grab at things. At six months most babies will be able to sit up with help and turn their heads around. They can pick up toys and like to put things in their mouths.

By nine months most babies can crawl. They can also hold a cup or bottle. Some may even stand while holding on to something. At twelve months lots of babies start to walk and say a few words.

Growing Up

In the first eighteen months of their lives, children experience their first growth spurt, and they grow very quickly. As their growth slows down between eighteen months and five years, they learn more physical skills and become more coordinated. From age seven on, swimming, ball sports, bike riding, dancing, and skating all become easier as a child gets more control over its body.

A second growth spurt happens at puberty. Puberty is the time when a child's body starts becoming more like an adult's and when the reproductive organs start growing and getting ready to work.

Puberty

Most girls start noticing changes in their bodies when they are between eleven and thirteen years old. However, some may notice their bodies changing when they are as young as nine, and others not until they are fifteen. This is all normal.

When a girl reaches puberty, hormones in her blood —estrogen and progesterone—tell her body to start changing. Her breasts start to grow. She gets a more defined waist and her hips start to look a little wider and more rounded. Pubic hair usually starts to grow in the area between and just above a girl's legs.

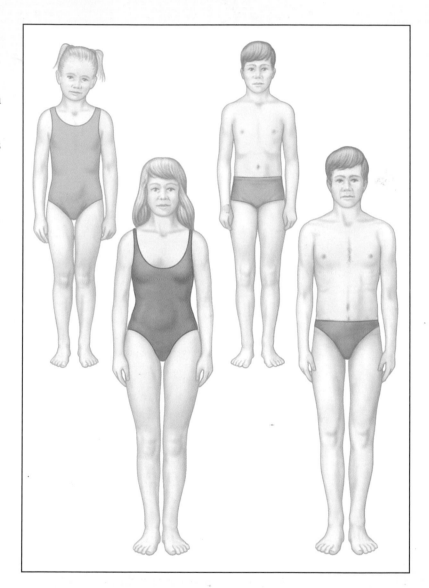

Growing up—before and after puberty.

Many teenagers get worried about acne appearing on their faces, but doctors are often able to help get rid of pimples.

Hair grows on her legs and under her arms as well. Her periods are likely to start around this time, too.

Boys tend to reach puberty a couple of years after girls. Their bodies also change. Their muscles get bigger, their voices get deeper, and they start to grow hair under their arms and in the pubic area, too. Boys also grow hair on their faces, legs and arms, and sometimes on their chests. At this time the male sex hormone—testosterone—is telling the boy's reproductive organs that it is time to produce sperm.

Case notes

Why do teenagers get acne?

Not all teenagers get acne, but many do. This is usually caused by the extra hormones in their bodies. These can cause more oil, called sebum, to get into the pores of the skin and clog them up. This clogging causes bacteria to multiply and this causes acne. Doctors and dermatologists (doctors who specialize in skin care) can help to make the acne better with special medicines.

Relationships and Feelings

A human being's world is full of different relationships and feelings. The first relationships babies and children are likely to experience are strong feelings of love from parents, brothers and sisters, and other members of the family. They then meet people outside the family. Friends, teachers, and doctors are just some of the people that children form relationships with as they grow up.

Relationships that make everyone involved feel trusted, respected, and cared for can be described as successful or healthy relationships. A relationship in which someone feels forced to do something they don't want to do, or that they know is wrong, can be described as unhealthy. Anyone involved in an unhealthy relationship should ask someone they trust for help.

Sexual Relationships

Sexual relationships are an important part of being human. Reproduction cannot happen without sexual intercourse taking place. It is natural for people to feel sexually attracted to one another.

It is also normal for these feelings to start at some point during puberty. When the reproductive organs start working, they release hormones into a

Wanting to be close to another person is a normal and important part of growing up.

young person's body that can make him or her feel attracted to another boy or girl. They may want to hug and kiss that person and be as close as possible. These feelings are natural, but they do not mean that someone who has reached puberty is ready for sexual intercourse and a baby.

Sometimes peer pressure from friends and classmates can make young people feel that they should have a sexual relationship before they are ready. Some people may even make up stories about how they have had sex with someone when they have not, to make themselves seem grown up and experienced.

In a healthy relationship, no one should ever feel forced to do something they do not want to.

Case notes

What is a homosexual relationship?

Not all relationships are heterosexual—between a male and a female who are sexually attracted to each other. A homosexual relationship is when two men or two women are sexually attracted to each other. These relationships are sometimes called gay relationships. When two women are sexually attracted to each other it is called a lesbian relationship.

Like other successful or healthy relationships, a good sexual relationship is built on trust, respect, and care for the other person's feelings. These relationships are built up over time.

Being pressured into having a sexual relationship too early and before both people are ready can result in unhappiness and an unplanned baby.

About Birth Control

Men and women who do not want an unplanned baby can use contraception—also known as birth control.

Condoms

These are a method of birth control that men can use to stop a woman from getting pregnant. A condom is a tube of thin rubber, closed at one end. It fits over an erect penis before it goes inside the vagina. Condoms catch sperm when the man ejaculates. Men and women can buy condoms from many different places, including pharmacies and supermarkets. They are available free at family planning clinics. There are also condoms for women, which fit inside the vagina. These can be bought from pharmacies, too.

Birth Control Pills

These are prescribed by doctors and contain hormones that stop the woman's ovaries from releasing eggs. Instead of taking pills, women can be injected with these hormones or have them implanted into their bodies. There are also emergency birth control pills that usually must be taken within seventy-two hours of having sex without using contraception. These are called morning-after pills and can either be prescribed by a doctor, or, in some countries, can be bought from a pharmacy.

Contraceptive pills are a very effective method of birth control if they are taken exactly as prescribed.

Doctors are very experienced in giving advice on birth control to young men and women.

Intrauterine Device

An intrauterine device (IUD) is a small, specially designed object a doctor puts into the uterus. IUDs stop sperm and eggs from joining together.

Diaphragm

This is a small plastic cap. It fits over the cervix to stop the sperm from getting into the uterus. Doctors can make sure that the diaphragm fits over the cervix properly.

Other Methods of Birth Control

The withdrawal method involves the man taking his penis out of the vagina before he ejaculates. This method is not recommended by birth control experts because the man may find it hard to withdraw and some sperm may come out before ejaculation.

The rhythm method of birth control involves not having sex around the days when the egg is ready to be fertilized. This method cannot be guaranteed to prevent pregnancy. The time for fertilization can be hard to predict and sometimes ovaries release more than one egg each month.

Sexually Transmitted Diseases

Sexual relationships are a normal part of human life, but sometimes they can make people ill. Diseases spread by sexual intercourse or by touching people sexually are called sexually transmitted diseases (STDs).

Pubic lice are parasites—tiny six-legged creatures that live in pubic hair. Special creams and lotions prescribed by a doctor will get rid of them. Pubic lice are also called crabs.

Syphilis, gonorrhea, and chlamydia are STDs that are caused by bacteria infecting the sex organs. Both men and women can become very ill from these infections. Infected people can be treated with medicines called antibiotics. Untreated STDs can cause inflammation of the female reproductive organs, which can lead to infertility or an ectopic pregnancy (the development of a fertilized egg outside the uterus, for example in a fallopian tube).

Other STDs are caused by viruses. Herpes is an infectious virus that causes sores on and around the sex organs. There is no cure, but medicines can make the sores go away for a while. Another virus causes genital warts. Although the warts can be treated, they usually grow back again.

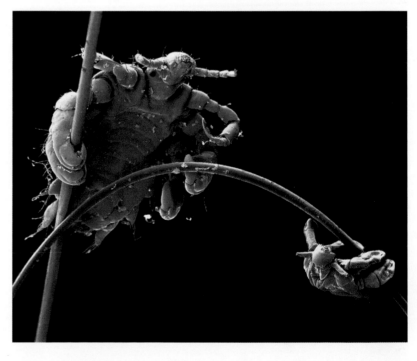

Pubic lice, also known as "crabs," live in pubic hair and are spread through sexual contact and poor hygiene.

Hepatitis B is a virus that spreads by sexual intercourse, by a person coming into contact with infected blood, or by being passed from mother to baby during pregnancy. It affects the liver and can make someone who has it very ill. There is no cure for hepatitis B, but there is an effective vaccine (a preparation that can stimulate the body's immune system to fight the disease). Most people who have it get better eventually.

Throughout the world, people are campaigning for, and trying to find, a cure for HIV/AIDS.

HIV/AIDS

HIV (Human Immunodeficiency Virus) causes a very serious STD. There is no cure, although scientists are working very hard to find one. HIV can live in someone's body for years without making them ill, but eventually it causes AIDS—Acquired Immune Deficiency Syndrome.

Once someone has AIDS he or she becomes ill because his or her body can no longer fight infection. Eventually he or she dies.

HIV can live in semen or in fluids from the vagina. It can also be spread by infected blood. HIV cannot be spread by coughing, sneezing, hugging, greeting someone with a kiss, or shaking hands.

Case notes

What is safer sex?

Safer sex is also called protected sex. People can protect themselves from STDs by using a condom. Safer sex is also about being honest and respectful in a sexual relationship. People with STDs should always let their sexual partners know and do their best to protect them from disease.

Glossary

AIDS — Short for Acquired Immune Deficiency Syndrome. People eventually get AIDS if they have been infected with HIV.

amoebae — Tiny single-celled animals that live in water and soil. Most amoebae can be seen only with a microscope.

bacteria — Single-celled organisms that can cause disease.

blastocyst — A ball of cells that starts forming after a sperm fertilizes an egg.

cervix — The opening at the bottom of the uterus, which widens when a baby is ready to be born.

chlamydia — A sexually transmitted disease that is caused by bacteria.

chromosomes — Strands of information contained in the cells.

cystic fibrosis — An inherited disease that makes the body create too much mucus.

diaphragm — A method of birth control in which a small plastic cap is fitted over the cervix to prevent sperm from reaching and fertilizing an egg.

DNA — Deoxyribonucleic acid. A chemical that makes up chromosomes and carries genes.

embryo — The medical name for a baby during the first eight weeks after fertilization.

estrogen — A female sex hormone.

fallopian tubes — The tubes that link the ovaries to the uterus, down which the eggs travel to be fertilized.

fetus — The medical name for a baby that has been in the uterus for longer than eight weeks.

genes — Packages of information attached to chromosomes that decide what characteristics a baby will inherit.

genital warts — A sexually transmitted disease that causes warts to form on the genitals (the external reproductive organs).

gonorrhea — A sexually transmitted disease caused by bacteria.

hemophilia — An inherited disease that stops blood from clotting properly.

hepatitis B — A sexually transmitted virus that affects the liver.

herpes — A sexually transmitted virus that causes sores to form on the genitals.

HIV — Short for Human Immunodeficiency Virus—infection with HIV is a serious sexually transmitted disease for which there is no cure. Eventually it causes AIDS.

hormones — Chemicals in the body that make things like birth, puberty, and menstruation happen.

IUD — Short for intrauterine device—a method of birth control in which a doctor inserts a small device into the uterus. An IUD is designed to prevent a sperm and egg from joining together.

muscular dystrophy — A hereditary disease that makes the muscles smaller than normal and unable to work properly.

nutrients — The parts of food, like vitamins and minerals, that are important for growth and development.

parasite — An animal that lives on and feeds off another animal, causing it damage.

placenta	The organ connected to the wall of the uterus during pregnancy that provides the baby with oxygen and nourishment.
progesterone	A female sex hormone.
reflex	An automatic action rather than something that is learned.
sebum	An oil produced by the glands in the skin.
syphilis	A very infectious and dangerous sexually transmitted disease. If left untreated, it can kill the infected person.
testosterone	The male sex hormone, produced by the testes.
umbilical cord	A cord that links the placenta to the baby's abdomen. It carries nourishment and oxygen to the baby.

For Further Exploration

Books

Hair in Funny Places
by Babette Cole (Red Fox, 2001)

Let's Talk About Sex: Growing Up, Changing Bodies, Sex and Sexual Health
by Robie H. Harris (Walker Books, 2004)

The Period Book: Everything You Don't Want to Ask (but Need to Know)
by Karen and Jennifer Gravelle (Piatkus, 1997)

Ready, Set, Grow!
by Linda Davick (New Market, 2003)

Reproduction and Birth
by Angela Royston (Heinemann, 1996)

Reproduction and Growing Up
by Steve Parker (Franklin Watts, 1998)

Understanding the Facts of Life
by Susan Meredith and Robyn Gee
(Usborne, 1996)

Web Sites

www.avert.org
An international AIDS charity.

www.cfoc.org/411AboutSex
Contains very good information on STDs and other topics.

www.iwannaknow.org
The American Social Health Association.

www.kidshealth.org/teen/sexual_health
Contains useful information on all aspects of puberty and sexual health.

www.talkingwithkids.org/sex.html
Contains advice about sex and relationships.

www.teenwire.com
The Planned Parenthood Federation of America.

Index

Page numbers in **bold** refer to
illustrations.